I'LL BE THERE SOON

This book is for Richard Arno Greene, 1932 -2015

Uncle, Physicist, Friend.

I'LL BE THERE SOON

JOHN WING JR.

Black Moss Press
2016

Library and Archives Canada Cataloguing in Publication

Wing, John, Jr., 1959-, author
    I'll be there soon / John Wing Jr.

Poems.
ISBN 978-0-88753-560-4 (paperback)

    I. Title.

PS8595.I5953I45 2016   C811'.54   C2016-901116-X

Editorial and Design Team:
Emily Anderson, Bibi Hijab Balkhi, Taylor Campbell, Brianna Craig, Maria Diakantoniou, Natasha Gaspar, Brittney Miller, Blake Van Dongen, and Katina Vido

Black Moss
EST. 1969 Press

Published by Black Moss Press at 2450 Byng Road, Windsor, Ontario, Canada, N8W 3E8. Black Moss books are distributed in Canada and the U.S. by Fitzhenry & Whiteside. All orders should be directed there.

Black Moss Press acknowledges the support of the Canada Council for the Arts and the Ontario Arts Council for its publishing program.

 Canada Council Conseil des arts
for the Arts du Canada

 ONTARIO ARTS COUNCIL
CONSEIL DES ARTS DE L'ONTARIO
an Ontario government agency
un organisme du gouvernement de l'Ontario

PRINTED IN CANADA

Acknowledgements

This book was edited by myself, and a team of editors including: Marty Gervais, Christina Angeli, Emily Anderson, Bibi Hijab Balkhi, Taylor Campbell, Brianna Craig, Maria Diakantoniou, Natasha Gaspar, Brittney Miller, Blake Van Dongen, and Katina Vido.

Don Coles and Steven Mayoff did early reads and edits of the manuscript, supplying much needed advice and encouragement. Rachel Wing and Dawn Greene also read much and suggested plenty, for which I am grateful.

Thanks also to, in the order my memory finds them, Greg Kennedy, Howard Nemetz, Tom Sobel, Luisa and Ron Beram, Robin Williams, Mark Pitta, Anton Leo, Ralph Benmergui, Doug Annear, Graham and Hilary Hadley, Glenner and Maria Anderson, John Yoder, the late Bill Sacra, David Quammen, Jeannette and Howard Aster, Nick Warner and Lisa Novick Warner, Paula Wing, Richard Wing, Isabel Wing, Valery Kalemba, Marc Chretien, Alexa Wing, Joe Rosenblatt, Phil Hall, Judy Shiner Toker, Angela Wing, Anthony Wing, and John M Wing, Sr.

Because I dislike mailing poems and waiting months to find out why they were simply not suitable for this or that periodical, none of these poems have ever appeared anywhere but here.

— John Wing Jr.

"It was a fantastic feeling, but it left me restless because the most important thing in it was the longing, for what was going to be, not for what I did or had done."

— Karl Ove Knausgaard

CONTENTS

Selective Memory I 9

Circus People 10

Occam's Razor: Fourth Grade 12

Old Habits 14

L'École À La Maison 16

Letter From a Burning Building 17

Sins 19

Killer Set 21

Selective Memory II 23

Road Stories: I 26

Luisa 29

Who You Marry 33

Distant Fire 36

Sometimes In Comedy 38

The Comedian 40

The Writer 41

Dad At 85 45

Road Stories: II 47

That Was The Year 51

Hourglass 53

Selective Memory III 54

Kids 55

Lullaby 56

Portents 58

Desire 59

In Two-Four Time 62

Selective Memory IV 63

Epiphanies 64

Harold: 1983   65

Transformation   67

The Swimmers   70

Gone or About to Be   71

The New Black   76

The Grateful Dream   77

Home: Old & New   78

Selective Memory V   79

SELECTIVE MEMORY I

Selective memory
is what people call it.
Psychiatrists like the phrase.
But memory isn't selective.
What the doctors are
talking about is lying.

Sometimes memory selects,
but not to give you a choice.
Something happens
and there's a line,
an image, something sticky
that adheres to the bank wall
and stays
with you
until death,
like a barnacle.

CIRCUS PEOPLE

The girl is pretty, nice legs shown off
in a mini-loincloth and dancer's shoes.
She goes out into the light carrying three
hula hoops, and kicks them, one by one,
into a spin on her body as music plays.
The first one to her knees, then she gyrates
and it rises to her waist, at which point
she kicks another one to the knee position,
lifts both of them at once, oddly thrilling,
waist to armpits, knees to waist, and finally
a third kick and she has three going round her
in many tight circles.

We all do something for a living.
In early school it's brought up
and each child makes a public prediction.
Some, confident in firm belief of future
achievement, say doctor, and many of those
little shits actually do become doctors.
Some are shy to say something so momentous,
so final-sounding, and have to be prompted,
"A lawyer, like your father?" Others make
obvious jokes: chewing gum taster, lingerie salesman.
But no one ever says 'insurance adjustor'
and I didn't say 'comedian.'

I asked the hula hoop girl, whose act
lasted four-and-a-half solid minutes,
what she foretold on that morning
in front of the whole class. She said
she was an eighth generation circus
performer. Her mother walked the wire.
Did she know? Did she say in a clear voice
audible to everyone, *Acrobat? Trapeze artist?*
Was she home-schooled under a big top,
instructed in the contortive arts by Dad?
Her future was predestined. She learned
very young to grow a beard.

I knew what I wanted then.
I wanted to be famous, and this
was back when it was very hard to achieve.
I didn't say it, because it wasn't a job;
it produced nothing of real value.
Still, the idea burned brightly within.
But I didn't want to be laughed at, rebuked
by the teacher, who resembled a female prison guard,
and would certainly tell my parents how foolish I was
at the next conference. *What are you going to do,
Mr. Wing?* she would have asked, *run off
and join the circus?*

OCCAM'S RAZOR: FOURTH GRADE

One day, the teacher had a flat map
of the world covering the blackboard,
and she drew a straight line from Halifax
to London, England, and then a curved
one that went over Greenland and Iceland
to London. "When planes fly to London,"
she asked, "which route do they use?"

Hands went up, she chose one. "Straight
across?" "No," she said. "They go the curved way.
Why?" "The wind, maybe? Is the wind stronger
going straight across?" "No," she said.
"So they won't be over water the whole
way?" "Nope, not that, either. None of you
have any idea?" Then Joey raised his hand.

"Yes, Joseph? Why do they fly that way?"
And Joey said, "Because it's shorter."
And not in a querulous, I-wonder-if-I'm-right
way. He stated it as a plain fact. Because
of the twenty of us, he alone could look
at a flat map of earth and see it
spherically.

The teacher beamed. "I never hear a peep out
of Joseph," she said, "but he knows things
the rest of you don't. He is destined for greatness."
But she was wrong. He ended up on the docks
loading and unloading ships, a muscle job.
Pick up and carry over. Point A to point B.
Simple solutions.

OLD HABITS

And now I am young, seven or eight,
and Dad has sent me to College Variety
to buy cigarettes. The variety store
seems obsolete today, but once it ruled
the little corners of our little towns.

Cigarettes, cheap cigars, candy – my God –
so much candy, pens, paper, small tools,
ice cream treats in a big box freezer, cold pop
that tasted as good as anything you would
ever drink, comic books, real books in swivel
racks, magazines with ladies in them, bare naked.

He has given me money and told me to keep
the change for myself. It is usually twenty cents,
which can buy a full bag of candy. My brother
saves his two dimes when he goes, but he's a fool.

The conversation is always the same; I say, *Two
packs of Philip Morris please, Mr. Buscemi.*
And he gives them to me, saying, *These for
you fadder, eh?* And I nod. He speaks with
an accent and sometimes my brother and I
imitate his cadences and laugh.

The packs are a medium beige-brown, and open
with an ingenious pull of silver paper. I bring them
to Dad, carefully hiding my candy bag in my bulging
back pocket. He opens the pack expertly, taps it
against his fingers to worry one out, and lights up.

The smell is wonderful. He unfolds the evening
newspaper with a snap, crosses his giant Dad-legs,
and commences reading, smoke curling up
above the paper like a secret fire.

L'École À La Maison

We weren't home-schooled.
We were home-dentist-ed.
A stout piece of string was tied
to the tooth with loose morals.
My father would pull it taut,
take out a cigarette, put it
in his mouth, pull out his
lighter, flick it on, and start
to light the smoke, before
thrusting the flame right
into my face without so much
as a *Look out, stupid*. When
my head snapped back into
place, the tooth would be
dangling at the end of the string
in his hand, the taste of blood
in my mouth mingled with smoke,
a curiously tangy combo the buds
recall even now. And I had
a quarter coming, with which
I would buy more gum. But no,
we weren't home schooled.

LETTER FROM A BURNING BUILDING

Dear Girl I Loved In High School,
I dreamt about you the other night.
We were sitting in the trombone section
of the band room. You were wearing
your purple and yellow knit socks
and your hexagonal specs. And the feeling
of small contented ecstasy was there, also.

Sitting next to you and being in love with you...
My wife said I sighed your name, and asked
if it was a sex dream. When I said it wasn't,
she replied, "You don't have to lie."

The dream was trying to tell me something
with images of you: in class, smoking
a cigarette in the alcove behind school,
playing trombone, the slide flashing
gold, your embouchure perfectly kissing
the mouthpiece. Maybe it was a sex dream.

You telling me we could only be friends, letting
me down easy. You at graduation. Then they faded
and I thought it was over, but you appeared again,
trombone in hand, beside me, smiling a little.
"You know I'm gay, right?" you said. And I did.
Or at least, I do now, forty years later.

You never said it to me then; such things weren't
discussed outside the psych office. But you wanted
me to know. I also knew it wasn't
the reason we never got together. I wonder if
I ever come into your dreams and say,
"You know you're why I write?"

SINS

Mr. Dillon arrived at our cruel-peak.
Probably no more than twenty-three, just
out of teacher's college, ten years
and a million nautical miles from us.
We were eighth graders, top
of the long, stupid tree.

Thirty of us, girls wearing
their first bras, boys bursting
to understand. And he, equal parts
idealism and exasperation,
guiding us through
puberty's swamp.

Some of us were nice,
but not me. Made a girl cry
in gym class that year, teasing
her loudly until the laughs stopped
and everyone was looking at me.
It's part of my punishment.

Hung a nickname on a big kid
that got picked up, went viral.
I called him 'Cow' and that became
his name away from home.
He should have kicked
the shit out of me.

He never shook the name, killed
himself with a rope at age 19. Found
his grave a few years later and left
some apologetic flowers. Tried to say
something, but what? *Sorry?* His first
name was the same as mine.

One morning in April, we were
informed by the principal that
Mr. Dillon had 'retired' from teaching.
Maybe if we'd been better behaved
he might have stuck it out. Maybe
others would still be alive.

KILLER SET

1974: The courthouse elevator,
smelling of good suits and fate.
Dad said to the police detective,
"This is my son, John. He wants
to see a murder preliminary."
Nods and smiles.

It was a nineteen-year-old boy
who had kidnapped two ten-year-old
girls and killed one. The other got away
and testified that day. Dad defended the boy,
who looked like angry Jesus and just
stared straight ahead all day, never looking
at anyone or changing expression.
I mentioned how creepy that was
on the way home, and Dad said,
"He acted that way on my instruction."

It was all over our school
how this crazed, fire-setting
animal killer had finally
serialized, and should now be,
in the words of a classmate,
"shot and hung."

Trial: Summation day.
Dad spoke to the jury, asking for
not guilty by reason of insanity,
and then the crown attorney got up
and told them he agreed.
The defendant was clearly not in full
faculty. The judge instructed that there
could only be one verdict.
After they'd been out for thirty-five minutes,
the crown attorney came over to Dad and asked,
"Should we call them back in and have the judge
read the instructions again?" Then they came in.
Not guilty. Insane. On the way home, I asked
what would happen to him. "He'll be sent to
a hospital," Dad replied. "For life?" I asked.
"Most likely."

1986: Hamilton, Comedy Club.
After my show, I am approached
by a homely couple. "Killer
set," the husband says, and asks
if I'm the son of the lawyer with
the same name from such-and-such,
and I say indeed I am. "Please send
my best to your Dad," he says,
and gives his name.

SELECTIVE MEMORY II

Paula Adele

Sometimes I think of how straight
a line the Maxwell street sidewalk
was that day.

And the tall Italian boy my sister was yelling at
turned. He seemed far away.

I think I knew he was a bully; every time
it's recalled, I have the same unease as he
turns and his arm comes up.

He's calling something out, and now he throws
a stone, a zip-bolt of silver shooting from his hand,
and I see it all the way until it strikes the center
of my forehead.

Pain is not memorable. Shock is. Fear.
Blood in my eyes. I'm screaming
as my sister drags me the block and a half
to our house. I'm six years old.

The cut will require stitches. Two,
perhaps? Four? No more than that.

But the memory usually ends with
the blood and the running home.
And the screaming. I could really scream then.

Each time it comes up, I try to find the aftermath.
The getting home, the trip to St. Joe's Hospital.
I was probably frogmarched
there with a towel held to my head, but no
recollection of it survives.

I write this because the other evening, nodding
off on the sofa, it came in semi-sleep, the silver
stone blasting me open, conscious, and I saw
something new. My sister.

Age eight, possibly viewing her first real
blood-gush, and scared, which I could feel
in cold sweat and short breath-coughs.
A fear we all carry. A knowledge-fear.
It's my fault; they'll blame it all on me.

But she doesn't panic. She tells me it's going
to be all right. Shepherds me home, the evidence
of her crime streaking my face. She who's
known me longer than anyone. I should call her.

And I do. Find a photo on Google Earth
of the street corner where it happened and send
it to her. She listens to the whole story, the whole poem,
then admits she has no recollection of it.

"My childhood is a blank," she says. I mention the name
of the bully, and she recalls him. "Yes! That dark Sicilian
danger boy! Probably a pizza delivery man today.
A broken man. A man without a good shirt."
We laugh about what I remember and she doesn't.

Later, I ask my mother if she remembers it,
and she doesn't either. She had five kids;
going to the hospital for stitches must have been
a weekly occurrence.

ROAD STORIES: I

As I get older, nothing scares me more than being confident that I know what I'm doing. As I was driving the Canadian route from Sarnia to Windsor one fine day a couple of years back, I got a bit lost in Chatham when I made a questionable turn onto a street I'd never been on before. I was trying to find the 401 and should have known the way, but I got bollixed up and ended up in unfamiliar territory. Along the way of this street, I passed a mini-mall. Within the small cadre of shops and offices, there was one that caught my eye. Burt Calvar Insurance. Burt Calvar, really? No.

In high school I knew a kid named Burt Calvar. "Burton James Calvar II," he would say, "But please call me Burt." He wasn't particularly tall, but he carried himself tall and more importantly, he dressed tall. Medium-length blond hair, blue eyes, nice clothes. Chicks dug him. He was the first of us that I knew who had a girlfriend outside of school. There was a coolness about him. He never spoke loudly, he never bragged, he never rushed. I once saw him walk into a hockey game at Sarnia Arena without a ticket. He actually nodded to the guy at the gate, and the guy let him in. He had said to me, "Come on, I'll get us in." But I was too embarrassed to try. He shrugged and I watched him walk right through. Burt was some guy. He was also one of the few of us who had a job. He worked at the men's clothing store downtown. He sold me my first suit, my graduation suit, and I was his customer and his admirer while he did it. I still remember parts of the pitch and the close. Not that it was difficult. I walked in knowing I was going to buy a suit, but Burt gave me the full Monty, and I appreciated it. We actually went out to dinner once in senior year, and I was so impressed with how he dealt with the waiter, always speaking quietly, always acting so goddamn *adult*. Just as I wanted to be.

We lost touch after high school, but neither of us were going to stay in a backwater town like Sarnia. We were going places. I went to Windsor for two years and then Toronto for eight more, and finally Los Angeles, where I settled. I had another friend who went to Toronto for a while, then changed careers and went to Honolulu, flourishing there for fifteen years, building up a damn fine business, and then selling it all at age fifty and moving to London, England, where his wife had a great opportunity. Life takes you, and you have to be willing to go.

• • •

I did my business in Windsor, and the next day I headed back to Sarnia.

But on the way I found myself back at the little mini mall again. I had to be sure. I pushed open the door to Burt Calvar Insurance to find a secretary, suitably young and fetching, greeting me. I asked if Burt might be in, and she said no, but he was on his way and expected any minute. Was I a customer?

"No," I said. "I think he's someone I knew in high school. Is Burt about fifty-three years old?

"Exactly right," she said.

"Is he about five ten with blond hair?"

"Indeed he is."

"Is he originally from Sarnia?" She wasn't sure about that. She'd never asked where he was from. I asked if she had a photo of him, and she was rooting around in her desk when he walked in. I turned and said, "Is that Burton James Calvar the second?" And he laughed.

"John Wing! How the hell are ya?" We went into his office. He looked good. Hair was still blond, maybe a little white in spots. He had something of a paunch, but nothing a diet and six weeks of good workouts wouldn't fix. There were photos on the wall of his wife and kids, and golf outings, four guys smiling their drunken asses off and the big 'Burt Calvar Insurance' sign behind them.

• • •

We sat there for forty-five minutes or so talking about our lives and he was still the same Burt. Cool, calm, quick to smile. After we talked, I got up to go, and he was very nice, said my next time through I'd have to come and have dinner, which of course was never going to happen. I had smiled and we'd shared a few minutes of nostalgia, but my larger, awful purpose was to prove it to be true: that I *was* better. I thought you were the coolest guy in high school and now you sell insurance in Chatham? Really? How did I think you were so cool and I was so lame back then?

Driving away, I felt like an asshole. Who was I to judge him? He got what he wanted. So did I. Good on us. If there's a moral to this, it's probably don't be the coolest guy in high school. And don't go looking for him, either, after all these years.

LUISA

When I was eleven,
I fell in love with a girl
who was also eleven. I suppose
it would have had more power if
she'd been fifteen, or even twenty.
But she was eleven.
A mature eleven.

The school we attended
had a large utility room in the basement,
and one day they took us downstairs
and we square-danced. She was my partner
for no reason that I remember, and
slightly sweaty by the third or fourth
pass-twirl, and by the fifth, I was
in love with her and it would never
be the same. Life would go on, yes,
but now I knew what love was, so
it could never go on as it had.

And some days or weeks or months
later, I have no idea because time
passed much differently then, I told her
that I loved her. Over the phone.

We'd held hands by this time, you understand.
Things were very serious, but I still
had trouble saying it. Not because
the words "I love you" or "I think
I love you" are inherently difficult to say.
Not at all. They fall out of your mouth.
The difficulty is that their power demands
a response, and that response cannot be
predicted.

And at eleven, I had probably
never thought of saying something
and then not said it. But the first
and the second time the phrase
occurred to me, with her right there,
some force stopped me. The words
refused.

So rather than risk her surprise and/or
revulsion face to face, and she had a lovely
face, I said it brokenly, over a tortured
several seconds on the phone one evening,
sitting on my parents' bed in their room
upstairs, the only semi-private phone in the house.

And while she was not put out or angry
at my revelation, or even surprised,
now that I think of it, she did not say,
"I love you, too," which is the ultimate goal
of all who dare the phrase. That it will be
instantly echoed, as though the person
hearing it had only been waiting.

I recall and can produce her exact words,
but wonder if they're really important
to what we're discussing here.
They were neither a rebuke nor an
affirmation. I was still to be held hands with
and perhaps even kissed, although memory
affords no taste of that anymore.
Mature elevens only go so far.

Years later, long after she'd
disappeared from my ideas,
my father and I were watching TV
and he described a woman on
the screen as a "high-voltage broad,"
and I knew exactly what he meant.
Luisa created current.

She'd moved away late in my eleventh
year and we'd lost touch very quickly.
But for some karmic reason, we met again
almost twenty summers later. She was married
by then. Her husband was the boy she met
the year after she'd moved.

He was a lawyer.
She was an archaeologist.
I was a comedian.
Somehow, it had all worked out.

I told her she was the first girl
I ever said "I love you" to. He probably
said it to her face, when they were dancing.
He twirled her, and she was perspiring
a little, and her hair, blondish from
a summer in the pool, was shiny and she
had that I-know-what-you're-thinking
smile on her face. Yes, no doubt he said it
to her face when they were dancing.

WHO YOU MARRY

Has more to do with your ultimate happiness
or unhappiness than any decision you will ever make.
And I know some of the early choices seemed so
momentous — school, career, where you would live —
but you always underestimated your adaptive properties;
you could live anywhere, other than the OneStopLight-ville
you hailed from. No, the crux is the mating, the choosing,
the dance to the sprint to the long walk. Don't mind me,
boys, just browsing for someone I can stand to be
in the same room with forever.

And it isn't sex. I'm very sorry to say it, but it's not.
In fact, I'll go as far as to say if you found the right
person *and* the sex was also fantastic, then I don't like you
and won't invite you to my card game. Because everything
fades; the first taser of being in love, the passion, even
the early idea that you have to hide those things she might
not like about you, plus what you're probably hiding
from yourself. Eventually, you grow weary of concealment
and are coaxed out of your mind's crawlspace,
blinking in the yellow safety of her light.

Also, choosing the right person doesn't mean you won't
go eye-wandering, either, stray off into the greenery
of someone else's garden. You might not, and my *God*,
it'll be easier if you don't, but weathering a few storms
can make a tree stand stronger, and other silly-ass metaphors
some high priest thought of while wrenching off his
collar at the end of a day. Fully understanding
what you have and why it's not worth any risk,
despite your pleading groin, takes maturity,
a state most men don't reach until their seventies.

And you don't fall into being a team right away – twenty-five
years of painstaking individuality jettisoned in one go – no,
you come together, collide, rebound, reboot, push, shove, assert,
insert, insult, spark, snark, want, reject, respect, wrack, crack, admit,
take and give, making incremental steps around thrown-up obstacles
toward a place where you can love each other without wanting
anything else. A friend once said the difference between being
in love and loving each other was the conversation. In love, you say,
Hi. Heard you got up today. Loving each other, you say, *Oh yeah?*
Well fuck you! And then you paint the baby's room a soothing tone.

We staked out early territories and often retreated into them.
But we always found our collective thought process docking
in a vast, silent deep-space, and there was a peace, a trust in
the lights that seemed light-years ahead. And I say *I love you*
to her every day – out loud – not because she needs to hear it,
because I need it to remind me that this trip-companion,
who made me wait months, *months*, for first sex, who passes
out compliments like a banker at a busker's convention,
proves I made a good decision once and till death.
So I say, think hard, children, and for heaven's sake, be *lucky*.

DISTANT FIRE

I watch Dad smoking with great envy
in my heart. He pops it to his lips, lights
a match with trembling hands, and fires
that baby up. And I smell the taste I miss,
the taste I have always known.

I envy him because I miss smoking.
The first one, anyway. Nothing ever tastes as
good as the first one, and I'm including everything
in that statement, but particularly cigarettes. I quit
for the fourth or fifth time over a year ago.

I recently did the math. He's been smoking
for seventy-two years, which is roughly 26,300 days,
averaging forty a day, and that makes
over one-million-fifty-thousand cigarettes
smoked in his life.

He should get some sort of award
or be checked by a phalanx of oncologists
to find out why he's still alive, albeit
with one foot and virtually no leg strength.
At eighty-five, all he can reliably do is smoke.

And he's outlived all his non-smoking
friends, all his friends who quit except one,
and he's never had a heart attack, or a cancer
scare that wasn't in his own head. Sure, his
breathing isn't soft and easy anymore, but still…

Once when he was around forty, he took us
for a drive down to some lake. And we parked
and spilled out of the car, four of his five kids.
The youngest, a rambunctious type, hit the ground
running hard for the edge of the dock.

And the rest of us, who had never seen Dad
move quickly for more than a couple of strides
across a room, were mesmerized as he set off
on the dead run, catching his third son about five
feet from proving he couldn't swim.

He brought him back and set him down, his
wind coming back in great heaving whooshes.
And Mother scolded her little boy while we
waited for Dad to breathe normally again…
And we're still waiting.

SOMETIMES IN COMEDY

Sometimes in comedy, the audience is bad.
But very rarely. Almost never, in fact.

Sometimes in comedy, a new joke falls flat,
and you were sure it was great, but it bombed.
You're so sure of its potential, you try it
again, and again after that. And still it bombs.
Finally you give up and put it out to notebook
pasture. Perhaps in a year or two it will pop
up like a blue whale somewhere you've never
seen a blue whale and you'll notice something
in the spout that solves this temporarily
abandoned riddle.

Sometimes in comedy, the comic before you
does all the same premises you normally do,
and in the same order, too. The funny thing is
the night before he opened for you and didn't
do one single premise that stepped on yours
or even dovetailed, and then he stayed to watch
your show. Now, one night later, all his
premises make yours seem derivative,
a copycat. When you confront him about it,
he says, "Yeah, you reminded me of some jokes
I used to do." Your only outlet will be the satisfaction
that he ends up working at a Home Depot in
his forties, dressed in an orange apron.

Sometimes in comedy, there's no pop
in the pop machine down the hall, and
no ice in the ice machine, and the TV
doesn't come in really well and it's
just that you're in Toledo.

Sometimes in comedy, a girl walks up
after the show in a purposeful way that
just sets your heart a-ticking, and when
she arrives in your very open after-show
space, she begins to tell you how much
of a misogynist you are and how she
wouldn't be surprised if you ended up
raping some poor girl and going to jail
for it, which is the best she could hope
for you. And you thank her.

Sometimes in comedy, you have to go
searching for the owner after the last show
in order to get paid. And after you find him,
he acts as though it's a large inconvenience
to pay you, since what you do looks so easy.

Sometimes in comedy, the show
is not right, the crowd is not laughing
in the right spots, or enough,
and you take deep breaths
and wonder
if it's you.
And it is.

THE COMEDIAN

for Robin Williams, 1951-2014

The media will lead with it for three days.
In-depth coverage, a whole half-page!
The funeral will be a star-studded affair;
Who's doing my black suit? How much will
an aisle seat cost me? Who's he wearing?

Roughly a year ago, in a theater
green room, pacing around to get my energy
level up from torpor, he came in. Fresh
from a film shoot, just off the plane,
smiling and calm as a heron.

That was the strange part.
He wasn't *on*. Just one of us,
a mutant, someone who never quite
fit in anywhere. A comedian enjoying
the safety of a room full of peers.

What a shame, will be the first thought.
Then reports will dwindle to hashtags
and trending lists; he'll be one of us again.
Someone who needed the sound, and
understood the space silence makes.

THE WRITER

I first saw him in the summer of 1980,
at the corner of Yonge and Charles.
Tall and round-headed, black hair
in a bowl cut, and a rabbit's face.
The nose prominent, the mouth small,
lips always pursed in mild annoyance.
A sign hung around his neck, saying
in bold letters, "Extremely Unpopular
Writer – Buy My Books." At his feet,
a bulging book bag.

We were competitors that summer.
Two blocks south, I was busking, playing
guitar and singing with an open case at Yonge
and Wellesely, partly because it had excellent
traffic in all directions, and partly because I was
in love with a girl who passed by around 5:30
each afternoon on her way to the subway.
When she finally saw me – and then only because
I called her name – she was shocked,
and never passed by again.

Soon I was a security guard
at the Manu-Life Centre at Bay and Bloor,
perhaps the only thing in this poem
that's still where it once was.
Heading to work, or heading home,

I would see the street author almost every day.
I had no money to buy his books, of course,
but I noticed some of the titles as I walked by.
Blood-Sucking Monkeys of North Tonawanda
always caught my eye.

By 1984 I was making what might be termed
a living at standup comedy, and my bank
was a Canada Trust on Bloor near Bay.
The author had begun to vary his selling spots,
and some days I would encounter him
right outside my bank, where we met formally.
His name was Crad Kilodney, and despite his
ready scowl and intimidating manner, he was a very
nice fellow once you got him talking. I bought
my first book from him that year.

It was called *Lightning Struck My Dick*. How could
one not buy a book with that title? He'd started breaking in
some new signs as well. One said, "Dead Brain Stories,"
another, "Literature For Mindless Blobs," and still others,
"Rotten Canadian Literature," and my all-time favourite,
"Slimy, Degenerative Fiction." I only saw that sign once.
Crad later confessed it had turned people off
and he sold nothing that day. I understood that.
Some jokes, no matter how funny they seemed to you,
never connected and had to go. Basic showbiz math.

Our routine became seeing each other on the street
between three and five times a year. A stop, a chat,
and a purchase. I bought *Pork College, Suburban
Chicken-Strangling Stories, Putrid Scum, Excrement,*
and one lucky day he had a copy of *The First Charnel
House Collection of Bad Poetry.* Charnel House was
the imprint under which he self-published all his titles.
He had once been the poetry editor of a small magazine
and he'd kept all the really bad submissions. One of which
began, "If Elvis was a goalie, stopping pucks for God..."

Were we friends? I don't know. We never met
anywhere but the streets of Toronto. We had a
professional relationship, I suppose. I made my
living in a slightly odd way, and he made his living
in a truly odd way. Ten or twelve years older
than I, he was a curmudgeon, while I was merely in
training to be one. I thought him a very brave man,
and wondered a lot where he found time to write,
and what gave him the dark sense of humour that
produced *I Chewed Mrs. Ewing's Raw Guts & Other Stories.*

I left Toronto for good in 1988. Returning
occasionally for work and family, I would
see him once every two or three years,
cruising an old downtown corridor.
The last time, probably 1996, he said he was
getting married to a woman who had children
and would be giving up street sales. I was happy

for him, and to show it, I bought his newest,
Foul Pus From Dead Dogs. This purchase ended
the physical meeting phase of our friendship.

His death made the social media pages
and the Toronto papers. The words cranky, notorious,
bizarre, and cult-figure were bandied about. They all
noted that he was the only writer ever to be arrested
and charged with selling his own work without a license,
a claim to fame I'm sure he enjoyed, being almost
Dickensian. We also found out Crad Kilodney was an
alias, and he'd been born in the U.S. Fitting, I suppose.
I wondered if his *nom de plume* was an anagram, but two
hours later decided no, it wasn't. Rest in peace.

DAD AT 85

The conversations are short now.
I can tell by how the pickup sounds
if it's him. Two rings, connect,
and a slow moment before his
austere, elderly, "Hello?"

How's business? How are the children?
Moments spent on each are newsy and brief.
If it's baseball season, we might
have a comment-minute on a game
or a player. "He's a great hitter…"

Today I asked what he thought
of our team this year – season starts
in two weeks, all promise still
possible – and he said, "They look
pretty mediocre to me."

Sometimes I save a joke to tell him,
but it has to be perfect, because
his silence at the end of a poor
choice is as chilling
as when I was a boy.

But he's there. At the end of the same
number, the same house, for forty-nine years.
And he's always happy I called.
Says my name, his name for me;
the one no one else has ever used.

ROAD STORIES: II

The Yoder circuit ran through Michigan, Ohio, Indiana, Illinois, and Wisconsin through the 1980's. John Yoder booked comedians from those states and many others, and each week working for John followed the same pattern. You'd do bar one-nighters Monday, Tuesday, and Wednesday, each in a different town, usually one with a college. Then Thursday through Saturday you'd be in a comedy club in one of the larger towns, Lansing, Grand Rapids, Kalamazoo, Madison, etc.

One autumn, probably circa 1986, I was doing the Lansing run, and the first stop was a motel in Owosso. A cheap motel. The kind that had one long bungalow and parking places right in front of each door. This particular Tuesday, I was first into the motel and the only customer. It was a warm day and I was standing by my open door having a smoke when another car pulled in and parked two rooms away. The driver door opened and a guy got out. His name was Bill Sacra, pronounced Say-cra. Although we'd never worked together (and after that week, we would never work together again), I recognized him immediately from the photos that papered the walls of every comedy club in the midwest.

I was about to wave to him but then the passenger side door of the car opened, facing me. It was strange, because I hadn't noticed anyone in the passenger seat. I still couldn't see anyone as the door opened, until a very small pair of legs appeared under the door and dropped to the ground. Okay, Bill travels with his kid. Unusual, sure, but okay. Maybe a divorce, or his wife died or went to prison or something. Then the small person came fully into view, and he wasn't a child. He was an adult little person.

By this point, for reasons I don't completely understand to this day, I was watching from behind my door, spying on them. I didn't want to be seen gawping at the little person, I guess. It was odd, certainly, but there were plenty of explicable scenarios, right? They were friends, maybe. Maybe they were related. He might be

Bill's drug dealer. After all, it was the 80's. Bill checked in at the office and they both went into a room.

At the show that night, Bill and I met formally, and he introduced me to, as he put it, "...my friend Joe." Joe hung out with us for a bit, had a drink, and then when the show started, I noticed he went and found a seat in the audience. We had a local host who was getting between thirty and fifty dollars to do ten minutes off the top and really suck, which he did very successfully. After exactly ten minutes of chatting and bad jokes, he introduced Bill, who would be doing thirty minutes. Bill had an almost New York rhythm act, although I'm pretty sure he wasn't from New York. His style was brash and confrontational and he had a lot of what I would call mean confidence. He never smiled.

About ten minutes into the act, somebody started heckling him. Not odd for a Tuesday night bar gig in Lower Michigan, certainly, but I remember finding it odd at first. Something was weird about it. The heckler was really laying it on, very loudly.

"Man! You're not funny at ALL!" was the first salvo. Bill seemed to take it in stride, which was also odd, since a really personal heckle can sometimes throw you for at least a moment. Not Bill.

"Oh, yeah? Well, you're an ASSHOLE!" Of course it got a big laugh, and Bill continued, "And now I AM funny, and you're STILL an asshole!" Which got a roar, and put the crowd totally on Bill's side. It seemed a little contrived, at least to me, because it was too perfectly timed. And on cue, the heckler chimed in again.

"Don't quit your day job, loser!"

Bill's reply was lightning quick: "Hope you can FIND one, fuckhead!" Another roar and a small applause break.

And it continued like that for two more heckle-retorts, and finally Bill, who couldn't see the heckler, fell into the trap.

"Why don't you come on up here and show me who you are so I can pound the shit out of you?"

Now, dealing with hecklers has many pitfalls, but this is the worst. To let your anger make you say something you regret. There is a courage that the adrenaline of being on stage gives you, and it can sometimes present itself as physical courage, which I have personally found is almost always a mistake. Bill was a bit bigger than I, and he certainly looked tough, but if you haven't seen the guy heckling you, you never know. Also, inviting someone up to share your stage is, to my mind, ALWAYS a bad idea. I can control what's happening on my stage when I'm there alone, but not when there's someone with me.

The heckler accepted Bill's challenge with a loud, "You BET, buddy!" and came up to the stage. And his getting on the stage got the third giant laugh. For of course, it was Joe the little person. Bill looked him up and down, which didn't take long.

"You probably think that I'm not gonna pound you into the floor just because you're a midget, right?"

"I think you're one of the biggest assholes I've ever seen!" Joe replied.

"Sure," said Bill, "But you think everybody is pretty big, don't you?"

And so it went for a couple of minutes, getting some good laughs. I was fascinated by where they would take it. How do you finish a bit like this? I went through a number of possible scenarios, but as I did, it began to get really weird. Bill was relentless in his verbal assault, and Joe began to weaken in his. Finally losing it entirely, he burst into tears, rambling in a barely coherent way about his mother and his awful childhood. The audience got very quiet, which I thought would bring Bill back to reality. It shows you how powerful it was, since I knew the guy was a plant and I still got sucked into it. But Joe's well-acted tears didn't stop Bill. He continued his harangue, finally ordering Joe from the stage and the establishment.

"Get the fuck out! You creepy little dwarf motherfucker!" Joe walked out, crying and rambling. It was some sort of surreal performance art, and you have to remember, we were in a college bar in Owosso, Michigan. Bill did about ten more minutes and said goodnight. I did my forty-five minutes, and when I finished, Bill was gone. When I got back to the hotel, I didn't go knock on their door, because I might have to share my marijuana with them, and I preferred being alone, anyway. When I awoke to check out and drive to Big Rapids, they were gone. And they never showed up in Big Rapids. Another comedian, Steve Iott, was there, saying he'd gotten a last minute call. I wondered if Bill had had an emergency, or somebody from the bar had called the booker and complained.

I never saw Bill again on the circuit. Many years later, I came across his name in an article about a show in Lake Tahoe. It was a 'copycat' show, and Bill played Rodney Dangerfield. I made a mental note to get out to see it the next time I was booked in Tahoe. But I never did. And then I heard he got cancer. And he died at only forty-six. He was only in his mid-twenties when we worked together. He seemed much older. So did Joe.

THAT WAS THE YEAR

That was the year the June bugs came in April.
The crops grew so fast we ate corn twice that summer.
Even the seventeen-year cicadas that sound like
South African sports horns decided it was too weird
to come out and changed their cycle to thirty-four years.
When they finally appeared, I was married and living
thousands of miles away.

That was the year we stopped using miles
and switched to binary sky-distances. When
the people next door moved away so early
one morning that no one saw them go. The house
was put up for sale, and the first real estate agent found
a rotting corpse in the upstairs bedroom.

That was the year the rainstorm knocked over
the tree in front of Mrs. Dudek's house, and it blocked
the street for two days while we played Moby Dick.

That was the year a newer, younger man became
our leader and we thronged to greet him when he
helicoptered in for a quick condescension.

That was the year they told us a Russian nuclear
strike would certainly target Detroit and we would
be collateral damage, and I had a dream of us speeding
the skyroad north to somewhere the fallout wouldn't reach.

That was the year winter never came and the river
didn't freeze and hockey season ended in September
and I scored a goal, my only goal, in that one game
that never counted because that was the year.

HOURGLASS

This is time: it has colours that bleed into ideas.
In yellow summer, there is an older boys'
baseball game one evening, and my brother
and I attend. We are told to be home at nine.
We don't wear watches and it's a long walk back,
but we manage to stroll into the den as the clock
strikes the ninth hour. My father is so impressed
that our first lesson becomes *Being on time pleases your father.*

A long time ago, I was twenty, or twenty-four
(my way of counting time was more haphazard then),
and the two rules of my job were *Be on time*
and *Do your time.* Oh, and how much time can you do?
How much do you have? It was something you built up
and measured yourself against, like the growth rings
of a doorway.

Time is the rare gift that is given as it is taken away.
Yet there are long minutes, short hours, swift decades,
absent friends who ran out. And my father, who was alive
the last time we had a winter like this one, marks his
couch-days in short breath and long memory, weighed
down by numbers, staring at the hourglass TV.

SELECTIVE MEMORY III

Memory is a balm,
a healer, sometimes
a jolter, an alarm bell
in your deep space psyche.
Remember me? Yes!
I still live here, deep in
your little coward heart.
Evidence upon request!

Memory is a bastard,
a sniper, a shaman
playing tricks. But who
can you trust if not
your own damn memory?
Unless it's your wife
saying, *How many?*
Not that many.

KIDS

When they're
small, tiny
bundles of amazement,
you write
about ambition:
what they will
become.

When they
appear grown,
deceptively,
you write
about their
youth: what
might have been.

Lullaby

Once, I saw her fall asleep,
saw the moment, the mechanism.
The eyelids dropped into darkness
and the baby girl was gone.

I was playing her a song
on the guitar, singing it softly,
looking right at her. *If I had
a boat, I'd go out on the ocean...*

During the second verse,
If I was Roy Rogers... she
clicked off her consciousness
and I kept playing.

Her crib was in a bedroom
she shared with her three-year-old
sister, who was already wishing
for her own damn room.

She reminded me of the vow
when she was eight, and we
moved to a house with rooms
for everyone. But I remember

the small bedroom they shared
for five years. Where I sang
that Lyle Lovett song that knocked
her sister out.

PORTENTS

The doctor, almost as an aside,
remarked, *Mental illness runs
in families, you know.*

Once such a sentence enters your head,
rattling around the high-score areas
like a pinball, it never leaves.

Even in your proudest moments, hard
work and achievements spattered with
applause, the phrase lights up

like a billboard that flashes
through the allergenic window
of a cheap hotel.

Your uncle's face appears, too.
His once-full Victorian beard now
stringy, matted with medical testimony.

Maybe it skips a generation
becomes a mantra; maybe it won't
come looking for me.

But then you had children, who
taught you fear the way no one
ever had before.

DESIRE

Flew to Nashville, paid off the landlord,
filled the car we gave her, and set off home.
She'd been gone ten weeks.

When I entered the apartment we'd found
for her, I was struck by its emptiness. She never
bought a table, or even a chair. "Let's go," I said.

Couldn't see out the rear view, it was
packed so tightly with boxes and dead ambition.
We did five hours that day, to Little Rock.

The previous spring, at dinner one night,
she said, "If I don't get into USC, maybe
I'll just go to Nashville and write songs."

Having done a similar thing myself at age twenty,
I applauded the idea. We made a plan, secured
an apartment, and gave her a car for the adventure.

Being eighteen makes your mind want something
until it's offered, and then you don't want it anymore.
She left home with a brave smile and too much fear.

Her depression deepened in the first weeks.
Never one to make fast friends, she wouldn't
perform anywhere, either. "I don't have any

songs," she would say. When I pointed out
that was a lie, she said, "I hate those songs."
Lyrics were begun but none finished.

After six weeks, my wife was so fearful
of her mental state that she told her she could
come home, as soon as one of us was free.

I understood why. A clear view into what
my parents must have gone through. It took
a month to clear the four days, and I went.

On the phone, she asked if the trip home
would be three days in the car listening to me
lecture her. "Pretty much," I replied.

The second day, I drove fifteen hours
across Texas to Las Cruces,
New Mexico, trying not to lecture.

We talked about everything but
the previous ten weeks, and it became
clear that she was really angry with me.

Turned out it was my fault. I wanted her
to be an artist so much. And she'd decided
she couldn't, and couldn't tell me.

We made it home the third night, thirty-three
hours driving total. Her presence now crowded
the nest, and for a while we tiptoed.

Every so often, she would get a look,
no doubt from seeing something on my face,
And her look would say simply, *Fuck you, old man.*

No one should ever be blamed for anything
they say or think at eighteen. She was right.
It was my fault. The wanting. The dream.

IN TWO-FOUR TIME

Too many people
in this house.
Too many dishes
and staggered wake-up times.

Two adults and two
children was pin-perfect,
two bathrooms and
a breathing room.

Now four adults and one
live-in, stay-over fiancé.
Too many buttons on
too many shirts.

Too many sandals
and fast food bags.
Too many night sounds
that can only be made by skin.

Selective Memory IV

We have reached the age where we teach
the almost-grown children of those we knew.
My sister teaches acting at a university,
and one of her students asks if I'm her brother,
because her mother went to grade school with me.

My sister says, "Yes, my brother was in love
with your mother when he was ten. She was all
he could talk about." (Apparently she's able
to recall *some* of that giant blank, her childhood.)
She asks our brother and he confirms my grade-five crush.

At graduation, a white-haired woman approaches
my sister. She leans in close and says, "I'm _____.
I loved him, too. I waited and waited for him
to ask me out but he never did." Her husband
comes to collect her.

My sister tells me the story, and its missed-chance
sweetness tears me up. "Of course I remember her," I say,
and I do. Big eyes, an enormous, welcoming smile.
"Mom remembers you being in love with her, too,"
my sister says.

EPIPHANIES

There is no light that flatters this body
anymore. Even a dim, red whorehouse
bulb leaves no doubt.

And this was not mentioned at all
by the clerks of my early education.
The save-it-for-marriage crowd.

Perhaps their reasoning was sound.
They might have known we'd simply
never believe such a thing.

For each of us, there was a moment
when they laid out some chilling little fact,
and you thought, *Oh, that is just horseshit.*

And then, the black corollary to the initial
rebellious notion kicked you hard.
What if it's all horseshit?

"Masturbation is a mortal sin, John,"
the priest said. "Every time you give in to it,
you are turning to the darkness."

You may have been right, Father, not that
it would have changed my path toward the light.
The electric one.

HAROLD: 1983

Those days, I often walked
home so late the night would
be dissolving into the gruff light
of morning, clear and cold. No
parents waiting up for me. Nothing
but being free.

Stoned, dragging on an Old Gold
one fall morning, a perfect night
of comedy and being rejected
behind me, replaying the conversations
in my spooled mind, I saw him.
Up ahead, a familiar flat-strided
lizard-walk, a head of permed blond
clown-hair, smile wide as a superhighway.
Hey Harold. Haven't we come a long way
from the theatre department
of a small university?

He was a dresser at O'Keefe now,
resplendent in a faux fox collared
coat. Lived near me. "Coming home
from a date," he said. "New boyfriend?"
I asked, and he grinned, maybe
just a touch ruefully. *Oh, you know,*
you meet, you fuck.

Sweet Harold died three years later;
the long way from college turned
out to be short. But it was a glorious
morning to be young in, even if
our souls were already marked 'sold.'

TRANSFORMATION

A friendship is not a marriage,
but it can be. There are things you must
accept, tropes and railings to let go,
in order that the friendship, the union that
you wish to keep, may thrive.

And within such a kinship, there are
moments of extreme calm, desperate
relaxation, when it never occurs to you
to think, *Who am I?* or *Why am I here?*
You can simply be. Together.

Which is, of course, why you value it
so highly, why you accepted all that they
were all those years ago, more than thirty now,
imagine. Because their love proved beyond
doubt that someone liked you, found you worthy.

And we change. The world gets bigger for some
and smaller for others. We each married,
had children who attained enough growth to
catch their own trains, and survived
into new decades of idea and ideals.

And then he left his wife, which was sad
and shocked us a little. Then he came out.
And while surprising, it at least explained
the first shock, and we took it in stride.
A new world for him, I thought, *and peace.*
And now, two years from his fifty-year-old
revelation, he has another. The word we use is
"transitioning." My friend tells us he's a woman,
and has a new name. And my acceptance has become
slightly arthritic. It has to stretch.

Because, of course, when someone says this, they
are also saying, "I've always been a woman."
When he told me he was gay, it wasn't like this,
because I wasn't affected by his being gay. So why
is this revelation more difficult?

Here are questions that never came up before.
Here I am doubting myself as she peels off old skins
and stops hiding. And I wonder what I must be hiding.
And it's not about lying or living a lie.
Hell, we all… let's not go there, either.

She was once a male friend of mine, and apparently
moving her into a new gender group, a smaller one,
is going to be too much work? Or is it I've always
known and loved her as a man, so why is she asking
me to change every idea of her I've ever had?

Because it simply doesn't occur to me to think
that I'll be asked for acceptance again.
I already did that. Complicated, and especially
shameful, that he and she would occupy such different
places in my personal hierarchy, or is it patriarchy?

Laziness. Or age. I don't like new, be it margarine
or novelists or people I was young with who tell me
I've been wrong about them since forever. Because
I don't like being wrong and it's generally all about me,
which was one of the things he accepted. And now she'll have to.

THE SWIMMERS

Meeting friends who have survived,
beaten back illness with gamma lasers
and plastic parts.

Pushing sixty, we walk slower
because the cart is heavy with
responsibilities and guilt-bricks.

But we are also new, having jumped
into the river all those days ago, allowing
the current to wash us up here tonight
on this restaurant shore.

When our parents were this age, they
were ancient, doddering, not even
trying to keep up.

We've kept our youth, cobbled from
graft and implant, cap and trade-off,
and the occasional performance-enhancer.

As the restaurant closes, we're flushed
with recalled strength, smiling in three
different directions, snug by a fire we built
a thousand short years ago.

GONE OR ABOUT TO BE

Dick went to UC Berkeley.
Studied nuclear physics.
Remember the nuclear bomb tests
on Bikini Atoll in '56 and '58?
Dick designed and built those bombs.

One of the complete sentences
he managed today during our visit
was about that. He looked up
at me from his bed, his eyes
sharp for that moment, and said,

"I used to build big bombs,
and I *loved* it." Then he drifted
away again, only able to say
single names, as though his mind
were a car with a dead battery.

He kept turning the key on
my name, hoping the sentence,
clearly formed somewhere in there,
could find the spark-charge
and drive right out of his mouth.

It's Easter Sunday at the old folk's home.
Dick is eighty-three. Seven or eight years ago,
a blood clot took his right leg, and after
the amputation, a stroke took most
of his intricate, bomb-designer brain.

He was so strong he survived it. After
therapy, he even got some speech back.
New aluminum leg and shoe, crutches,
walkers with wheels. They jury-rigged
him for more storms.

Under the covers, one full leg and one
stump are clearly outlined. "John…"
he says. "John, I'm…" his hands move
the covers down a bit, and I see
the edge of a diaper. "I'm wet," he says.

I go downstairs and tell the lady
at reception. I say he had an accident,
thinking it might bring a caregiver
faster. I go back upstairs to his room,
and no one comes.

I take his hand and we talk in our
telepathic guessing language. I look
at his wall, the photos of his dead wife,
and he notices and begins to weep.
"Why did Nancy have to die?" he asks.

I could tell him. His second wife faked lupus
for twenty years, and ruined her health with
the medication, because she was afraid
if she wasn't sick no one would pay any
attention to her. But I don't say it.

When he got sick, she was too far gone
to do any stepping up. And his children
hated her, and they all lived far away.
He's not even my uncle. He's my wife's
uncle. "Where are they?" he asks.
I go out and stare down two sides
of an empty hall. No place on earth is
quieter than an assisted living facility.
Back inside, I say, "It's Easter Sunday,
so it might be a while." "I'm wet," he says.

Twenty years ago, he was the foremost
American expert on Eastern European
nuclear capabilities. This broken, one-legged
man who can barely put four words together,
and weeps for lost love.

He was present at the birth of our first
daughter, a twenty-nine-hour labour marathon.
And as my wife was beginning to dilate
in earnest, I saw Dick, ringside,
trying to look anywhere else.

He and Nancy were de facto grandparents
to our kids for twenty years. Now they're gone
or about to be. Sitting with Dick, I realize
I'm roughly the same age he was
when we met.

I go down to reception a second time.
The elevator lists the day's activities.
The first one is 'Balloon Toss.' The girl
is young and wears a small nose ring.
I wonder if she's ever been upstairs.

Back in Dick's room, we resume our
hand-holding. I check the hallway again, in all
its yawning, rectangular, brown emptiness.
"Will someone come?" he asks, and as if I'm
not there, he calls to the door, "Help!"

No one arrives, and I have to leave.
I kiss him on his spotted head. He thanks
me for coming. I want to tell him
it will be all right, but he's not stupid,
so I don't. He waves as I go.

On the way out, I make a plea to the nose-
ring girl to get someone to help him. She
is sweetly reassuring. Lies flow like
honey from her lips. I want to warn her,
Don't get old, but it would sound ridiculous.

Home takes an hour, and immediately
after I arrive, Dick calls. "John…"
he says, "Help! You come… help… I need
you." "I just got home, Dick, and it will
take me at least an hour…" and he hangs up.

He calls again at four the next morning,
again saying help. A voice from the gone
world, the deserted brown corridor.
Sleepily, I say I'll be there soon, recognizing
that it has two meanings.

THE NEW BLACK

The children are leaving.
Two more weeks and they disperse
to the northeast. No more the path,
the drought-coloured yard, the cacti,
lemon, lime, loquat, and grapefruit tree,
the silk oak, the redwood, the bamboo.
The garage full of their early lives.

Off they'll go, prepared and unprepared,
adults in the new lightspeed world.
As they pack memories into boxes
to sit unopened until we die,
as the second leg of the journey
careens up like a drunken stallion,
we, too, begin again.

THE GRATEFUL DREAM

In the grateful dream,
there is a commotion downstairs
and I see Dad walk in on two fine, strong legs
and announce we have purchased a new sofa.

And I'm so thankful to see him walking,
remembering how purposeful and directed
his stride always was, how substantial
his presence.

The grateful dream recalls him in his vibrancy,
before stubbornness took his mobility
and engagement. He laughs, and I wake up
without even noticing how young I was, watching him.

Home: Old & New

This place
exists only
in your memory.

The town is not
what it once
was.

It's moved on
through time
without you,

like a lover
who married
and had children

that were going to be yours.
And they grew strong
in someone else's name.

"What brings you?"
they ask, stopping short
of naming you *Visitor*.

I usually answer, "I'm
writing a book." That
shuts them up.

SELECTIVE MEMORY V

What if everything
was not as you remembered?
Like the iced mornings you
rode a Ski-Doo out to a frozen
bay, and fished. What if
that wasn't you pulling up
that fat old perch, yellow
and black and *Ha! Look!*

What if the girl you loved
was so distraught by your
leaving town that she
killed herself, and no one
ever told you? What if
she didn't love you?
It was all pretense.

And the married woman
you had sex with the first
time, what if you hadn't
been awkward and rabbited
with fear? What if you looked
back on it with enjoyment
instead of shame?

What if they all
had a group on Facebook
called *I Never Loved
You Either*? All of them
swearing they'd never
even met you.

What if you dreamed
it up, wrote it down,
wrote it over, dined out
and parlour-pieced it
until you knew every beat,
and it was all complete
horseshit?

Well, then you wouldn't
be a poet, old man.
You'd be a novelist.

Author's Note

No book is perfect, thankfully, or there'd be no reason to begin the next.

The joke about love in "Who You Marry" was written (and performed) by Howard Nemetz, back in the 1980's.

If you recognize yourself in these pages, I hope I had the decency to change your name. I changed most of them. Left Paula Adele, my sister's name, intact. I guess I was reasonably sure she wouldn't sue me.

As always, the reminiscences are through my own, very peculiar, rose-coloured funhouse mirror, and if you don't recall the episodes as I do, I'm sorry.

"That Was The Year" was inspired by a memory of Gregory Banks Kennedy's high school epic poem, "Life Without June Bugs."

No book is thankful, perfectly, or there'd be no begin to the next reason.

About The Author

John Wing Jr. was born and raised in Sarnia, Ontario where he honed his love for poetry before his well known vocation. He moved to Los Angeles early in his career to expand his horizons and open new doors for his career. This move turned out to be crucial, not so much for his career, but for this newly formed family. His second home paved the way for his success both on stage and with his family. Even with all these homes he considers Windsor his spirit city.

Other books published by Black Moss Press:

Why-Shaped Scars
When The Red Light Goes On Get Off: A Life in Comedy